"I have a grandma named Great"

And Other Delightful Quotes
from Young Children

By Claire Ericksen
Illustrated by Mary Ericksen

Distributed by
ADVENTURE PUBLICATIONS
P.O. BOX 269
CAMBRIDGE, MN 55008
1-800-678-7006

This book is affectionately dedicated
to all the children who have attended
Northfield Day Care Center
and to the teachers who have
faithfully recorded their words.

Can you remember the vast and wondrous world of your pre-school years? It is a fragile place, too soon dissolved by experience. In that far-off land, eternity is just about as long as it takes to put on your own socks, a feast is a peanut-butter and jelly sandwich, an adventure is a walk around the block, and a best friend, a teddy bear.

It is a place still inhabited by three to five year olds, intent on discovering its secrets. Their confident comments and poignant conclusions, respectfully quoted here, provide both a wry glimpse of childhood today and a reflection of our own innocent beginnings.

Claire Ericksen

Table of Contents

"I'm the boss of myself, my doll and my dad."

Parents

"I'm the boss of myself, my doll and my dad."

"We only like girls that act like boys — and our moms."

"If you want to be a mom, you have to say 'no no no no no no.' "

"I went into the bathroom when my mom
was taking a bath and I saw her ticks."

(Argument)
"Mommy is my mother."
"No, she's my mother."

"When my dad shaved off his mustache,
his smile got bigger."

"I went to New York when I was still in my mommy's tummy
so I couldn't see very much. I just had to peek out the tiny hole."

"My mom's in bed with stitches.
Now we have to pour all the stuff ourselves."

"Santa is smarter than moms. He *knows* what kids want."

"When I whine, my mom says yes."

"This is a picture of me kicking, trying to get out of mommy's tummy."
"Well, why didn't you just climb out of her mouth?"
"Yup, that's what I did."

"We have a boy dad at my house."

"My mom's so smart. She can tie a double knot."
"My mom's not so smart. Sometimes when I'm fooling she believes me."

"My mom has chopped lips.
I wonder who chopped 'em."

"If your mom dies,
your dad has to have you in his tummy."

(Discussion)
"I don't have a cat but I used to."
"I don't have a dad but I used to."

"Mom, I wish you were four so you could come
to day-care and sit by me all day long."

(Child to mother)
"You go now. I'm trying to have fun."

"I went swimming all by myself.
Just me and my dad's head."

"Be quiet. I think I can hear the seeds shaking out of my head."

My Body

"Be quiet. I think I can hear
the seeds shaking out of my head."

"I don't need a jacket,
I can keep warm in my imagination."

"You have to have guts to be smart."
"Where are they? In your mouth?"
"No, they're in your body. Do you have any?"
"Yes, I have some."

"Look at this red stuff coming out of my skin.
Maybe it's blood."

"Yesterday I was electricity."

"I don't think this pee in my pants is mine."

(In the bathroom)
"It wasn't poop, it was just smoke."

"I can't see. I have a frog in my eye."

"I'm not wearing my pacifier today.
I'm just wearing my thumb."

"Oh oh, wet pants again.
I suppose you'll have to neuter me now."

"I think the air is coming out of my finger —
I need a band-aide."

"When I suck the blood out of my cut,
I die a little."

(A boy, feeling his chest)
"I feel a baby kicking."

"I went p-o-t-t-y in my pants."

"Both of my faces are cold."

"Don't wipe my face off.
I want my face on!"

"This potty is torturing my bottom."

"I have to tell you something very important.
I have a heart."

"I wonder why no one lives on other planets. There must be mean dogs there."

Thinking

"I wonder why no one lives on other planets.
There must be mean dogs there."

"We have two bathrooms in our house.
One in the house and one in the bush."

"I don't know where it isn't."

"I know how warm it is today — numbers."

"At nap, I think I can hear
the carpet breathing."

"The music is so beautiful
it makes me feel like crying."

"When I'm not talking, I'm thinking."

"I didn't bring my snow pants, but it's o.k., I have snow underpants on."

"Hey, I've got some of the letters from the alphabet in my name."

"You can see with your mind up in your head."

(Watching a bubble pop)
"It must have been scared."

"I'm tired and I'm bored and my underwear is fizzing."

"I can hardly wait to go to kindergarten —
but actually my stomach feels sort of funny."

"If my little sister falls out the window, we'll say: 'There she goes!'"

"I know where the bubbles are going.
They are going to pop."

"I like Santa Claus but
I'm sort of scared of his muscles."

"Wouldn't it be fun if people could dance to words?'"

"Now I'm on four,
but on my birthday I'll be on five."

"Ghosts aren't invisible —
you can see their sheets."

"That baby is crying too much. Shut her down."

"The leaves are falling. Some guy has to put them back up."

Gender

"The leaves are falling.
Some guy has to put them back up."

"I can't understand you because you're a boy."

"Homely girls, phooey.
What are boys to them?"

"That picture is so pretty, I think maybe a girl did it."

"I think boys should marry each other
so girls can really be left out."

"Don't say please.
It's a girl word."

"My penis was worried because I wanted to be
one of those girls in the pink dresses."

"I love it when girls tip upside down when they have dresses on,
because then you can see their fancy underwear."

(Boy)
"How is it like to be a girl?"

"A blouse is sort of a wibbley shirt for girls."

"Would you please get a calendar and turn me into a kitty?
I feel really weird being a boy all day long."

"I'd rather be a nerd than a girl."

"If you're going to be good, you've got be a girl.
Only girls are good."

"I wish I was a girl. Then I wouldn't be messy.
I'd be neat when I eat."

"Boys have brown guns and girls have pretty guns."

(Rejecting a boy)
"You can't play because you have brown hair
and we have girl hair."

(Whispering boys)
"Did you know the teachers are girls?"

"Girls kiss football players. Yuk."

"When I grow up, I'm going to buy me a wand
and turn me into a girl."

"I think my grandpa would like a paper doll of my grandma for Christmas."

Grown-ups

"I think my grandpa would like a
paper doll of my grandma for Christmas."

"Oh, teacher, I love you. You're so old and poor."

"I have a grandmother that is poor —
but it is not the rich one."

"Did you see that girl with gray hair? That's my grandma."

(Wiping his hand on teacher's skirt)
"Hi, towel."

"My grandpa drives very carefully
so he can stay alive until he's dead."

"I got a present from 'gram' somebody — oh yeah, gram ma."

"My mom went to a country where they talk like this:
'Would you like some more tea?'"

"The brown fell off my grandpa's hair.
Now it's gray."

"Teacher, how did you get to know everything?"

(To teacher)
"You're an old girl, aren't you?"

(Sitting on teacher's lap)
"Will you just say you're my mom, because that's who
I want right now, my mom."

"He can't see. He's bald."

"Those worker guys that make houses —
how do they make people?"

"I have a grandma named 'great.'"

"Teacher, you have too much skin."

"Artists always know what they're drawing."

"Why are so many people named 'Mister'?"

"She got married and then she was so tired
she went straight to bed."

"My uncle is 30 years old and his legs are 30 too."

"If you give me a parakeet for my birthday, you better not wrap it."

Friends

"If you give me a parakeet for my birthday,
you better not wrap it."

"When someone cries, it makes me hot."

"I hit her because she hit me back first."

"Here, you can wipe it up with my socks."

"When I didn't know her I thought she looked ugly,
but now that I know her I think she looks pretty."

"I wish you had a different head.
One with more of a smile."

"In this game, you have to be naughty."
"Okay, I'll be naughty. But I don't know what to do first."

"I'm so mean — and friendly."

"We have a secret — but don't worry. It's not very interesting."

"You can marry him as soon as I'm through marrying him."

"Don't bother me.
I'm only going to like hanging around with boys."

"First I'll change your diaper, then I'll sit on your lap."

"He's my friend. I hate him."

"Come on, let's be dead together."

"I want to play all by myself with somebody."

"You know what I hate about you?
You are riding the tricycle I want."

(About a quiet new child)
"Well, there are more things in life than talking."

"Don't laugh when I change my clothes and you see my underwear, right?"
"O.K. but I can smile, right?"
"Right."

(Listening to a child speaking Japanese)
"He can sure make a lot of music."

"Girls can't marry girls. They have to marry boys."
"Unless the boys don't like you. Then you can marry a girl."

"Playtime can't be over... I didn't even get a chance to eat the child yet."

Pretend

"Playtime can't be over —
I didn't even get a chance to eat the child yet."

"Now let's stop playing and start fighting."

"I'm the fire girl here and
I don't like to find pants on fire."

"These guys had such a big accident that even
the Republicans can't fix them."

"Well, just say I was cancelled."

"These Barbies get to be naked
because they live in France."

"Pretend you're a statue. Act fake."

"Well, shall we go to college
or shall we just sit around the house?"

"First, build a mountain."

"Teacher, save those blocks for me, because when I grow up
I'm going to make a spaceship and I'll need them."

"We were on our way to grandma's
when we heard 'tinkle tinkle'—
and all the babies had peed in their pants."

"Do you want to play 'sisters'? It's a real good game.
The mom and dad both died."

"Let's not play for real. Let's play pretend."

(Playing with Barbie dolls)
"If Ken marries two Barbies,
they can play ring around the rosey."

"I don't like this game.
Can't we play something more violent?"

(Plotting against a girl)
"Let's hit her in the wiener."

(To doll)
"Tell me right now. Why did you die?"

"I want something to wear.
And make sure it's indecent."

"Chi-chi-ching, chi-chi-ching. Can you hear my spurs?"

"There's no such thing as magic except on cereal boxes."

Edibles

"There's no such thing
as magic except on cereal boxes."

"I need a cracker, my mouth is hungry."

"I'm eating all the snow
so it will be summer."

"Say, can I eat your cookie for awhile?"

"Glory to God,
these graham crackers are so good."

"First you eat half, then I'll eat half.
Then you eat half and then I'll eat half."

(At lunch)
"Please pass the dead chicken."

"I turned a summer salt and pepper."

"A jelly fish eats jelly."
"No, a jelly fish makes jelly."
"No, a jelly fish is made out of jelly."

"Here's a candy heart for you. Don't eat it.
I hate peppermint breath."

"My favorite food is seconds."

"We're making sand soup with dinosaurs — it's junk food."

"I was gonna make some chocolate milk
but I couldn't find any chalk."

"Don't you love the way
sugar scratches your throat?"

"I know what one-a-piece means.
It means you can't have any more."

"When something is sour, you have
to eat it with one eye closed."

"I practically had to force my mom to make
cupcakes for my birthday."

"I love Wheaties. They're made from bread."
"No they're not. Weedies are made from weeds."

"Ducks wear rubber gloves on their feet so they don't slip on the ice."

Outdoors

"Ducks wear rubber gloves on their feet
so they don't slip on the ice."

"This is an Indian gun, it shoots stickers and prickles."

"I know another name for the deep part of the lake — bottom."

"Hail is little marbles that fall down and get you freezed."

"We found a swimming pool outside.
That's why our snowsuits are wet."

"I know how you can get some fur.
Just get a pail and put my cat in it and save her shed in the pail."

"I wish the sky would come down
so that I could see the corners."

(A cloudy day)
"What happened to the blue stuff?"

"I woke up because I heard a snowflake falling."

"I can smell the sun today."

"Do you think the sky really fell on Chicken Little?"
"No. The sky is glued up."
"No, it's taped up."

"The rain is a sky sprinkler."

(After the first snowfall)
"Hey, the grass is gone."

"What do you have in your garden?"
"A lot of sun."

(Foggy day)
"Hey, it's blurry out."

"Look, that tree has a nose."
"That's not a nose. That's a boob."
"No way. It's too big for a boob."

"We're putting nails in the dirt
so the worms will get sticked."

"When you get striked by thunder,
you explode."

"I know how many stars are in the sky. A lot. Maybe more."

Language

"I know how many stars are in the sky. A lot. Maybe more."

(Examining a tiny fiber)
"I think it's a fairy tail."

"Scribbling is a square word."

"Teacher, do you know any F words? I do, poop."

"You know where your tummy drains out?
That's where dirty words come from."

"Sometimes I sneak into my sister's room and scribble in her diarrhea."

"Fee-fie-fo-fum, I smell the butt of an Englishman."

(Skipping and singing)
"God, this is boring."

"A boy that used to come here swears on the school bus
and talks about sexy things like underwear."

"He said a word my dad knows: 'God.'"

"When you call somebody a *britch*
you are really calling them pants,
because britches are pants."

"I was scared out of my nit-wits."

"It's okay to say 'nerd.'
It isn't a swear word."

"Splinter is French for sliver."

"Old mother goose sat on her cupboard,
pulled out a duck and flied away home."

(Furious boy)
"You — you old bride!"

Girl: "Chugga chugga choo choo..."
Boy: "Hey, that's a truck."
Girl: "Okay. Trucka trucka troo troo..."

"Darn.
I forgot how to say those not nice words."

"You can't say 'Jesus,' but it's okay to say 'baby Jesus.'"

"'Damn' means you trip or something."

"My kitty is an angel now. She'll really flap her wings and catch all the birds."

Feelings

"My kitty is an angel now. She'll really flap her wings and catch all the birds."

"I didn't mean to do it. It was just on purpose."

"Why do moms and dads hate people?"

(Girl listening to distant ambulance siren)
"I hope there aren't any girls hurt."

"Our kitten died so we had to let it go."

"I'm so happy it makes tears come out of my eyes."

"Sometimes people feel sick, then they go
to the doctor or up to heaven."

"We have to listen very carefully to see
if someone says something we can't listen to."

"Do you want to hear something? In real life, you die."

"If I get really sick, I'll go up in the air,
but if I get better, I'll come back down."

"In heaven, your mom would never have to go to the office."

(After an argument)
"I hope my face doesn't show a smile."

"I have a grandma that I've never seen, but I have to love her anyway.
That's just the way it is."

"Sometimes when I say I'm sorry, I don't feel sorry at all."

(Angry)
"Well, when I grow up, I'm going to have a movie store
with no movies for anybody."

"As soon as I get to heaven, I'm going to come back down
and explode so I can be a ghost."

"I know how poor people can get food —
they can go trick or treating."

"I can't believe it. Some people speak Spanish."

"I always sleep with my eyes open,
so I can see my dreams."

"If God were a pickle, we'd all be pickles."

Philosophy

"If God were a pickle, we'd all be pickles."

"I did it, I did it, I did it. Did I do it?"

"I'm me. Right?"

"When you don't get any toys, then you swear."

"Do the days just keep coming?"

"Whoever wins, loses."

"I can't stop being happy."

"You can tell how much someone loves
you by how much they hug you."

"If you give something to yourself,
that's called keeping."

"The people she doesn't know,
she hates the best."

"On the day I was born, was everyone else born?"

"Why do poison berries look so sweet?"

"I'm not accidental.
I was meant to be."

"Why is it he doesn't like to get hurt when he plays with girls,
but he doesn't care if he gets hurt when he's playing with boys?"

"Taking turns, that's just part of life."

"I already died before, so I don't have to die again."
"Oh yes, you will. You'll see."

"Sometimes it seems I haven't been living very long."

(Amazed at receiving a catalog order)
"How did it get real?"

"When is then? Is it yesterday?"

"After you grow up, is there anything else?"

 Claire Ericksen has been director of a non-profit Minnesota day care center for 25 years, and claims to have enjoyed every minute (well, almost). Although now quite ordinary, she aspires to be a truly great grandma.

Mary Ericksen has an extensive resume of making art with kids of all ages. Her own work, influenced by the imagination and humor of a child's view of the world, is exhibited in shops and galleries around the country.